Shirlee Finley

PLANT BASED DIET COOKBOOK

ALKALINE FOODS RECIPES

*61 delicious, healthy and easy
recipes with Alkaline Foods
that will help you stay fit and detox your body
while respecting nature*

Table of Contents

Introduction

Alkaline foods are those whose residues not metabolized by the body have a basic pH, such as fruits and all vegetables. A proper alkaline diet is able to preserve the health of the human body and keep it in balance. Let's find out more about them.

The vital processes of the human organism require a stable and slightly alkaline ph. When the ph of the tissues is constantly on acid values, it means that an accumulation of acid toxins or a loss of basic elements (such as calcium and sodium) has occurred. Acidification of the biological terrain is the cause, or concomitant cause, of many symptoms and disorders (obesity and chronic degenerative diseases), reduces the efficiency of the immune system and promotes cellular aging. A proper diet that includes the daily intake of alkalizing foods and the reduction of acidifying foods allows to preserve the balance of the human body and health.

Alkalizing foods, in general, have anti-inflammatory, detoxifying, antioxidant, energizing and invigorating properties. They are also ideal to ensure the body the right amount of fiber, minerals and vitamins.

It follows that the benefits of a diet that tends to the correct balance between alkalinity and acidity can be summarized as follows:

- Strengthening of the immune system
- Improvement of digestive and intestinal functions
- Detox effect
- Prevention of cellular aging

An adequate alkalizing diet, except for particular needs that will be carefully evaluated by the doctor and nutritionist, must include about 80% of alkalizing foods and 20% of acidifying foods. Particularly acidifying foods are refined cereals that should be replaced with "whole" cereals (to be banned are refined flours and products obtained by mixing bran with refined flours), animal proteins, sugars, alcohol, coffee, some types of tea, precooked foods, foods with a high content of phytochemicals and chemical additives.

Alkalizing foods promote the right biochemical processes in our bodies and are rich in vitamins and minerals. These include seasonal fruits and vegetables, vegetable oils, oil seeds and nuts. In general, the following foods are considered alkalizing:

- all vegetables, including salads,
- potatoes (eaten with their peels),
- fruits (including sour fruits),

2

- dried fruits,
- almonds and cashews,
- alkaline mineral waters,
- baking soda,
- sea salt.

Especially alkalizing are the following foods: umeboshi plums, broccoli cabbage, seaweed, citrus fruits, pumpkin seeds, persimmons, watermelon, cinnamon, molasses, soy sauce, chestnuts, bell pepper, peppers, miso, kohlrabi, collard greens, garlic, asparagus, parsley, endive, arugula, green mustard, ginger, broccoli, nectarine, pineapple, molasses, cantaloupe, blackberry, mango.

ALKALINE
FOODS
RECIPES

1. Sebi Alkaline Strawberry Jam Recipe

Preparation time: 10 minutes.

Cooking time: 20 minutes.

Servings: 16 ounces.

Ingredients:

- 4 cups sliced strawberries
- 2/3 cups of raw agave
- 3 tablespoons of key lime juice
- 1/2 cup Irish moss gel

Directions:

1. Slice enough strawberries to fill up 4 cups.
2. Mash or blend to your desired texture.
3. Agave, lime juice, and strawberries should be added to the saucepan on high heat.
4. Cook for 10 minutes, then add Irish moss gel.
5. Cook for 5 more minutes to make certain that the gel has been thoroughly dissolved.

6. Remove from heat and allow the sauce to cool down before refrigerating.

7. Dish your alkaline electric strawberry jam!

Nutrition:

- **Calories:** 56
- **Carbohydrate:** 13g

2. Alkaline Mushroom Chickpea Burgers Recipe

Preparation time: 20 minutes.

Cooking time: 30 minutes.

Servings: 8

Ingredients:

- 2 portobello mushrooms
- 2 cups cooked chickpeas
- 2 teaspoons onion powder
- 2 teaspoons Himalayan sea salt
- 2 teaspoons oregano
- 1/2 cup cilantro
- 1/4 cup garbanzo bean flour
- 1/2 teaspoon cayenne
- 1/2 cup green peppers
- 1/2 cup red and white onions
- Food processor or blender
- 1/4 measurement cup

Directions:

1. Chop the mushrooms into chunks and dice the vegetables.

2. Place all the ingredients in a food processor and pulse for 3 seconds.

3. Check for consistency, if it's too wet, add more flour and then scoop into a bowl.

4. Set your cooker to medium heat and sprinkle grapeseed oil into the skillet.

5. Scoop the blend into a cup and turn it over to your cooking surface.

6. Allow the blend for 5 minutes on each side. Apply caution when flipping so that the blend can stay together.

7. Your alkaline mushroom/chickpea burgers are ready to be served.

Nutrition:

- **Calories:** 225
- **Carbohydrates:** 22.5g
- **Fat:** 14.2gs
- **Protein:** 11.4g

3. Alkaline Roasted Tomato Sauce Recipe

Preparation time: 15 minutes.

Cooking time: 40 minutes.

Servings: 6

Ingredients:

- 18 Roma tomatoes
- 1/2 red bell pepper
- 1/2 sweet onion
- 1/2 red onion
- 1 medium shallot
- 1/8 cup grapeseed oil
- 1 tablespoon agave
- 3 teaspoons sea salt
- 3 teaspoons basil
- 2 teaspoons oregano
- 2 teaspoons onion powder
- 1/8 teaspoon cayenne powder

Equipment:

- Blender
- Cookie sheet
- Parchment paper
- Pot—at least 4 quarts

Directions:

1. Preheat your oven to 400°F.
2. Chop the vegetables in half and place them in a bowl.
3. Sprinkle grapeseed oil and a teaspoon of both basil and sea salt.
4. Sprinkle the chopped vegetables in the mixture until it is fully coated.
5. Place all the vegetables on a cookie sheet.
6. Bake in the oven for 30 minutes.
7. Toss the roasted vegetables into a blender and blend at high speed.
8. Pour the paste and the remaining ingredients into a pot. Allow it to cook for 20 minutes.

Nutrition:

- **Calories:** 25
- **Fat:** 2g
- **Sodium:** 80mg
- **Carbohydrate:** 2g

4. Curry White Bean Cup

Preparation time: 15 minutes.

Cooking time: 0 minutes.

Servings: 4

Ingredients:

- 1 can white beans
- 1 garlic clove
- 1 tablespoon lemon juice
- ¼ cup avocado oil
- 3 teaspoons curry powder
- ½ teaspoon paprika
- Sea salt and black pepper to preference

Directions:

1. Add all the ingredients to a food processor and blend until smooth. Transfer to an airtight container and store in the refrigerator until ready to be consumed.

Nutrition:

- Calories: 280
- Fat: 14g
- Protein: 12g
- Carbs: 32g

5. Salt and Vinegar Chips

Preparation time: 12 hours and 10 minutes.
Cooking time: 10 minutes.
Servings: 8

Ingredients:
- 1 zucchini
- 2 teaspoons of olive oil, extra-virgin
- 2 tablespoons apple cider vinegar
- Himalayan salt to preference

Directions:
1. Preheat the oven to 110°F. Use a knife to slice the zucchini very thin. Turn the setting to 1/8. Add the zucchini to a bowl and toss in all other ingredients.
2. Pour the zucchini onto Teflon-lined sheets. Bake and dehydrate for 12 hours until crispy.

Nutrition:
- **Calories: 13**
- **Fat: 1g**
- **Protein: 0.5g**
- **Carbs: 0g**

6. Alkaline Veggie Fajitas Recipe

Preparation time: 10 minutes.

Cooking time: 20 minutes.

Servings: 6–12

Ingredients:

- 1/2 cups cut green and red peppers
- 1/2 cups cut red and white onions
- 3 cups cut mushrooms
- 2 teaspoons ocean salt
- 2 teaspoons onion powder
- 2 teaspoons sweet basil
- 2 teaspoons oregano
- 1/2 teaspoon cayenne powder
- Juice from 1/2 of a lime
- 2 tablespoons grapeseed oil
- Alkaline spelt tortillas
- Alkaline guacamole (discretionary)
- Alkaline mango salsa (discretionary)

Tip: If you would prefer not to utilize mushrooms in this recipe, you can essentially exclude them and cut each preparation in half

Directions:

1. Make your mushrooms, bell peppers, and onions into long strips.

2. Set your cooker to medium heat, then sprinkle 1 tablespoon of grapeseed oil on the skillet.

3. Sprinkle another tablespoon of grapeseed oil in a large skillet.

4. Mix your vegetables and seasoning, then sauté for 5 minutes.

5. Serve them on spelt tortillas with guacamole and salsa.

6. Your alkaline veggie fajitas are ready to be dished.

Nutrition:

- **Calories:** 257
- **Fat:** 2g
- **Saturated fat:** 0.4g
- **Protein:** 12.9g
- **Carbohydrate:** 50.3g
- **Sugar:** 8g

7. Alkaline Vegan Hot Dogs Recipe

Preparation time: 20 minutes.

Cooking time: 40 minutes.

Servings: 10

Ingredients:

- 1 cup garbanzo beans
- 1 cup spelt flour
- 1/2 cup aquafaba
- 1/3 cup green pepper, diced
- 1/3 cup onion, diced
- 1/4 cup shallots, diced
- 1 tablespoon onion powder
- 2 teaspoons smoked sea salt
- 1 teaspoon coriander
- 1/2 teaspoon ginger
- 1/2 teaspoon dill
- 1/2 teaspoon fennel

- 1/2 teaspoon crushed red pepper (optional)
- Alkaline electric ketchup (optional)
- Grapeseed oil for sautéing
- Alkaline electric buns (optional)

Directions:

1. Sprinkle grapeseed oil in your skillet, add vegetables and garbanzo beans, then sauté for 5 minutes.

2. Place the remaining vegetables and other ingredients in a food processor until it is well blended.

3. Scoop the mixture into your hand, then make hotdog shapes with them and wrap them with parchment paper afterward.

4. The molded hotdogs should be steamed for 40 minutes.

5. Once the steaming process is done, unwrap the hotdogs.

6. Sprinkle grapeseed oil in a skillet and cook the hotdogs for 10 minutes on medium heat.

7. Your alkaline electric hotdogs are ready to be dished.

Nutrition:

- **Calories:** 159.2
- **Carbohydrates:** 6.3g
- **Fat:** 3.3g
- **Protein:** 25.5g

8. Alkaline Quinoa Milk Recipe

Preparation time: 10 minutes.

Cooking time: 5 minutes.

Servings: 4

Ingredients:

- 1 cup cooked white quinoa
- 3 cups spring water
- 6–8 dates
- 1 pinch sea salt (optional)
- 1 pinch cloves (optional)
- Blender
- Milk bag or cheesecloth

Directions:

1. Make a perfect blend of these ingredients in a blender.

2. Sieve with milk bag or cheesecloth.

3. Enjoy your well-deserved Dr. Sebi alkaline quinoa milk recipe.

Nutrition:

- **Calories:** 111.
- **Sugar:** 3.2g
- **Sodium:** 5mg
- **Fat:** 1.6g
- **Saturated fat:** 0.2g
- **Carbohydrates:** 20.7g
- **Fiber:** 2.3g

9. Alkaline Avocado Mayo Recipe

Preparation time: 10 minutes.

Cooking time: 10 minutes.

Servings: 1 cup

Ingredients:

- Juice from half of a lime
- 1 avocado
- 1/4 cup cilantro
- 1/2 teaspoon sea salt
- 1/2 teaspoon onion powder
- 2–4 tablespoons olive oil
- Pinch of cayenne powder
- Blender or hand mixer

Directions:

1. Remove the pit of the avocado and scoop the insides into a blender.

2. Add the rest of the ingredients and blend at a high speed.

3. For hand mixers, add all other ingredients, except for the oil which should be added slowly until the desired consistency is reached.

4. Dish your alkaline avocado mayo!

Nutrition:

- **Calories:** 45
- **Fat:** 4.5g
- **Sodium:** 100mg
- **Carbohydrate:** 0.5g

10.Alkaline Spicy Kale Recipe

Preparation time: 10 minutes.

Cooking time: 15 minutes.

Servings: 4

Ingredients:

- 1 bunch of kale
- 1/4 cup onion, diced
- 1/4 cup red pepper, diced
- 1 teaspoon crushed red pepper
- 1/4 teaspoon sea salt
- Alkaline "garlic" oil or grapeseed oil for greasing
- Salad spinner (optional)
- **Note:** if you do not have a salad spinner, you can as well air dry the kale.

Directions:

1. Rinse the kale, fold its leaves into halves, and cut off the stem.

2. Chop kale into bits and remove the water using a salad spinner.

3. Set your cooker to high and add 2 tablespoons of oil.

4. Sauté salt, pepper, and onions for 3 minutes.

5. Reduce the heat to low, add the chopped kale, and cover for 5 minutes.

6. Crushed pepper should be introduced to the mix, stir and cover for another 3 minutes.

7. Dish your alkaline spicy kale!

Nutrition:

- **Calories:** 85.2
- **Fat:** 1.2g
- **Sodium:** 61.2mg
- **Carbohydrates:** 18g
- **Fiber:** 5.9g
- **Protein:** 5.3g

11. Alkaline Date Syrup Recipe

Preparation time: 10 minutes.

Cooking time: 15 minutes.

Servings: 16–24 ounces.

Ingredients:

- 1 cup dates, preferably pitted
- 1 cup of spring water
- This sweetener can be easily dissolved in water, unlike date sugar.

Directions:

1. Boil spring water, then remove it from heat when boiled.
2. Place dates in the boiled water for at least 5 minutes.
3. Pour the dates and some water into a blender, then blend until it's smooth.
4. If the texture is too thick, add more water and blend again.
5. Keep it in the refrigerator and dish with alkaline date syrup!

Nutrition:

- **Calories:** 270
- **Potassium: 848**mg
- **Sodium:** 5mg
- **Carbohydrates:** 67g
- **Fiber:** 3g
- **Sugar:** 61g
- **Protein:** 1g

12.Alkaline Buns Recipe

Preparation time: 20 minutes.

Cooking time: 1 hour.

Servings: 6

Ingredients:

- 2(1/4) cups—2(1/2) cups spelt flour
- 1/2 cup hemp milk or walnut milk
- 1/4 cup aquafaba
- 1/4 cup sparkling spring water
- 1 tablespoon agave
- 1 tablespoon onion powder
- 1(1/2) teaspoon sea salt
- 1 teaspoon basil or oregano
- 2 teaspoons grapeseed oil
- 1 teaspoon sea moss gel (optional)
- Sesame seeds (optional)
- Mixer with the dough hook

- Baking sheet
- Plastic wrap
- Parchment paper
- **Note:** if you do not have a mixer, you can knead by hand.

Directions:

1. Add all the dry ingredients into a mixing bowl and blend perfectly.

2. Add the remaining ingredients and blend at low speed for a minute. Then knead the dough at medium speed for 5 minutes.

3. Sprinkle grapeseed oil on a baking sheet already laced with parchment paper.

4. Separate dough into parts, roll with hand to make shapes, then place on baking sheet.

5. Brush the top with oil, then add sesame seeds.

6. Use a plastic wrap to cover the buns and allow it to sit for 30 minutes.

7. Set your oven to 350°F and bake for half an hour.

8. Allow the buns to cook and carefully cut them in half to enjoy your alkaline electric buns!

Nutrition:

- **Carbohydrates:** 47g
- **Fat:** 7g
- **Protein:** 9g

13. Vegan Onion Rings

Preparation time: 30 minutes.

Cooking time: 10 minutes.

Servings: 4

Ingredients:

- 2 sweet onions, peeled
- 2/3 cup all-purpose flour
- 2/3 cup almond milk, unsweetened
- 1 teaspoon garlic powder
- 1 teaspoon smoked paprika powder
- 1 tablespoon nutritional yeast
- 1 cup panko breadcrumbs
- ¼ teaspoon salt

Directions:

1. Preheat the oven to 350°F. Line a baking sheet with parchment paper. Combine flour, spices, nutritional yeast, and almond milk in a bowl. Stir well.
2. Place the breadcrumbs into a separate bowl. Cut the onions into ¼ inch rings and separate.
3. Coat each onion ring in the spices, then follow by dipping in the breadcrumbs. Lay the onion rings onto the baking sheet when finished.
4. Bake for 20 minutes. Remove the pan and flip each onion ring. Bake for an additional 10 minutes. Serve warm with additional dipping sauce if desired.

Nutrition:

- **Calories:** 200

- **Fat:** 1g

- **Protein:** 6g

- **Carbs:** 40g

14. Guacamole

Preparation time: 15 minutes.

Cooking time: 10 minutes.

Servings: 8

Ingredients:

- 2 avocados, ripe
- 1 tablespoon lime juice
- 1 cup cilantro, roughly chopped
- ½ cup red onion, roughly chopped
- ½ cup cherry tomatoes, quartered (optional)
- ¼ cup canned jalapeno peppers, chopped
- ¼ teaspoon garlic powder
- ¼ teaspoon cumin
- ½ teaspoon salt

Directions:

1. Add onion, tomato, jalapeno peppers, and lime juice to a mixing bowl. Sprinkle in all seasonings and stir to incorporate.
2. Fold in avocado chunks. Stir, but do not over-mix, to create a thick texture. Serve immediately over a salad, as a side, with vegetables, or with crackers.

Nutrition:

- **Calories: 110**
- **Fat: 10g**
- **Protein: 1.5g**
- **Carbs: 6g**

15.Easy Stovetop Bread

Preparation time: 15 minutes.

Cooking time: 10 minutes.

Servings: 4

Ingredients:

- 1 cup all-purpose flour
- 1 teaspoon baking powder
- 2 tablespoons olive oil
- ½ teaspoon salt
- 1/3 cup warm water
- ½ teaspoon rosemary
- ½ teaspoon herbs of choice

Directions:

1. Combine flour, baking powder, plus salt in a mixing bowl. Stir in olive oil and water. Stir until combined, but do not over-process.
2. Once oiled a skillet with olive oil, then warm over medium heat. Shape the dough into 4 patties. Drop the dough into the skillet. Cook each side for 5 minutes.
3. Sprinkle herbs on each side while cooking. Serve immediately or microwave when ready to consume.

Nutrition:

- **Calories:165**
- **Fat: 8g**
- **Protein:4g**
- **Carbs:23g**

16.Black Bean Dip

Preparation time: 15 minutes.

Cooking time: 5 minutes.

Servings: 6

Ingredients:

- 15 ounces (1 can) black beans, drained and rinsed
- 2 tablespoons red onion, roughly chopped
- 1 small tomato, chopped
- 2 teaspoons garlic, minced
- ½ teaspoon cumin
- ½ lime, juiced
- Himalayan salt to preference

Directions:
1. Add all the ingredients to a food processor and pulse until combined. Serve hot or warm. This recipe also makes a great dressing for salads.

Nutrition:

- **Calories: 70**
- **Fat: 0.5g**
- **Protein: 5g**
- **Carbs: 13g**

17. Oven Potato Fries

Preparation time: 15 minutes.

Cooking time: 30 minutes.

Servings: 1

Ingredients:

- 2(½) pounds baking potatoes
- 1 teaspoon vegetable oil
- 1 tablespoon white sugar
- 1 teaspoon salt
- 1 pinch ground cayenne pepper

Directions:

1. Start by preheating the oven by setting the temperature to 450°F. Take a baking sheet and line it with a foil. Spray the sheet with a generous amount of cooking spray.
2. Scrub well to clean the potatoes. Cut each potato into half an inch-thick strips.
3. Take a large-sized mixing bowl and toss in the potato strips. Add the vegetable oil, salt, cayenne pepper, and sugar.

4. Place the coated fries on the baking tray lined with cooking spray. Place the baking sheet in the preheated oven and bake for about 30 minutes. Transfer onto a serving platter and serve right away.

Nutrition:

- **Calories:263**

- **Carbs:35g**

- **Fat:12g**

- **Protein:4g**

18.Zucchini Stuffed with Mushrooms and Chickpeas

Preparation time: 30 minutes

Cooking time: 30 minutes

Servings: 1

Ingredients:

- 4 zucchinis (halved)
- 1 tablespoon olive oil
- 1 onion (chopped)
- 2 garlic cloves (crushed)
- ½ package button mushrooms, sliced (8 ounces)
- 1 teaspoon ground coriander
- 1(½)teaspoon ground cumin
- 1 can chickpeas (15.5-ounces)
- ½ lemon (juiced)
- 2 tablespoons fresh parsley (chopped)
- Sea salt, as per taste
- Ground black pepper, as per taste

Directions:

1. Start by preheating the oven by setting the temperature to 350°F. Take a shallow nonstick baking dish and grease it generously.
2. Use a spoon to scoop out the flesh in the center of zucchini halves. Chop the flesh into Place the zucchini halves onto the greased baking dish.
3. In the meanwhile, take a large nonstick skillet and place it over medium flame. Toss in the onions and sauté for about 5 minutes. Add the garlic and sauté for 2 more minutes.
4. Now add the mushrooms and zucchini. Keep stirring and cook for about 5 minutes.
5. Add the chickpeas, cumin, coriander, parsley, lemon juice, pepper, and salt. Mix well to combine.
6. Put the zucchini shells on your baking sheet and fill them with the chickpea mixture. Put the baking sheet in your oven and bake for about 40 minutes.
7. Once done, remove from the oven and transfer onto a serving platter. Serve hot!

Nutrition:

- **Calories: 149**
- **Carbs: 10g**
- **Fat: 10g**
- **Protein: 8g**

19. Vegetable Medley

Preparation time: 20 minutes.

Cooking time: 15 minutes.

Servings: 1

Ingredients:

- 1 tomato (diced)
- 1 pinch garlic pepper seasoning
- 2 fresh mushrooms (sliced)
- 2 yellow squash (cubed)
- Cooking spray for greasing
- 2 zucchini (cubed)

Directions:

1. Start by taking a large skillet and greasing it using the cooking spray. Place the skillet over medium flame and add the tomatoes.
2. Let the tomatoes cook for about 5 minutes. Add the garlic pepper seasoning. Toss in the mushrooms, zucchini, and squash. Let them cook on a medium flame for about 15 minutes. Serve.

Nutrition:

- **Calories: 49**
- **Carbs: 1g**
- **Fat: 5g**
- **Protein: 0g**

20. Mushrooms with Herbs and White Wine

Preparation time: 10 minutes.

Cooking time: 15 minutes.

Servings: 1

Ingredients

- 1 tablespoon olive oil
- 1(½) pound fresh mushrooms
- 1 teaspoon Italian seasoning
- ¼ cup dry white wine
- 2 garlic cloves (minced)
- Salt, as per taste
- Pepper, as per taste
- 2 tablespoons fresh chives (chopped)

Directions:

1. Start by heating the olive oil by placing the nonstick skillet on medium-high flame. Once the oil is heated, toss in the mushrooms. Sprinkle the Italian seasoning and sauté for about 10 minutes. Keep stirring.

2. Pour in the dry white wine and toss in the garlic. Continue to cook for about 3-4 minutes. Season with pepper and salt. Sprinkle the chives and cook for about a minute. Move into a serving bowl, then serve hot.

Nutrition:

- **Calories: 522**

- **Carbs: 27g**

- **Fat: 16g**

- **Protein: 55g**

21. White Beans with Collard Greens

Preparation time: 15 minutes.

Cooking time: 40 minutes.

Servings: 1

Ingredients

- 2 tablespoons water
- 1(¼) cup onion (chopped)
- 3 tablespoons garlic (minced)
- 1 cube vegetarian bouillon (beef-flavored)
- 7 ounces collard greens (chopped
- 14ounces diced tomatoes, no added salt (1 can)
- 1(¼) cup water
- Salt, as per taste
- Black pepper (freshly ground), as per taste
- 14(½-ounce) great Northern beans (1 can)
- 1 teaspoon white sugar

Directions:

1. Start by placing a large nonstick skillet on medium flame. Pour in 2 tablespoons of water. Let it heat through.
2. Stir in garlic and onion and cook for about 10 minutes. Add more water if required to avoid scorching. Add the vegetarian bouillon to the pan. Keep stirring.
3. Toss in the collard greens and tomatoes to the onion mixture. Also, add 1(¼) cup of water.
4. Season the mixture with pepper and salt. Cover with a lid and cook for about 20 minutes. Make sure that all vegetables become tender.
5. Now add the sugar and beans and cook for about 10 minutes. Serve.

Nutrition:

- **Calories: 251**
- **Carbs: 39g**
- **Fat: 3g**
- **Protein: 19g**

22.   White Beans and Avocado Toast

Preparation time: 5 minutes.

Cooking time: 1 minute.

Servings: 1

Ingredients:

- 1 slice whole-wheat bread
- ¼ avocado
- ½ cup canned white beans, rinsed and drained
- Kosher salt, as per taste
- Ground pepper, as per taste
- Crushed red pepper, as per taste

Directions:

1. Start by taking a toaster and placing the whole-wheat bread in it to toast. Once done, remove and keep aside. Take a small bowl and mash to avocado.

2. Take the canned white beans and thoroughly rinse and drain them. Place the toast on a plate and top it with mashed avocado.

3. Place the white beans on top as well. Nicely season with pepper, salt, and red pepper. Serve.

Nutrition:

- **Calories: 307**
- **Carbs: 37g**
- **Fat: 6g**
- **Protein: 14g**

23. Fresh Edamame Pods with Aleppo Pepper

Preparation time: 0 minutes.

Cooking time: 5 minutes.

Servings: 1

Ingredients:

- ½ cup Edamame (in pods)
- 1/8 teaspoon Aleppo pepper

Directions:

1. Start by taking a steamer and place it over a high flame. Fill it with water and let it come to a boil.

2. Place the edamame pods in the steamer and steam for about 5 minutes. The pods should be crisp and tender. Transfer into a serving platter and sprinkle with Aleppo pepper.

Nutrition:

- **Calories: 124**
- **Carbs: 12g**
- **Fat: 4g**
- **Protein: 10g**

24. Cabbage & Beet Stew

Preparation time: 20 minutes.

Cooking time: 10 minutes.

Servings: 4

Ingredients:

- 2 tablespoons olive oil

- 3 cups vegetable broth

- 2 tablespoons lemon juice, fresh

- ½ teaspoon garlic powder

- ½ cup carrots, shredded

- 2 cups cabbage, shredded

- 1 cup beets, shredded

- Dill for garnish

- ½ teaspoon onion powder

- Sea salt & black pepper to taste

Directions:

1. Heat oil in a pot and then sauté your vegetables.
2. Pour your broth in, mixing in your seasoning. Simmer until it's cooked through and then top with dill.

Nutrition:

- **Calories: 263**
- **Carbohydrates: 8g**
- **Protein: 20.3g**
- **Fat: 24g**

25.　The Mediterranean Delight with Fresh Vinaigrette

Preparation time: 5 minutes.

Cooking time: 10 minutes.

Servings: 2

Ingredients:

Herbed citrus vinaigrette:

- 1 tablespoon of lemon juice

- 2 tablespoons of orange juice

- ½ teaspoon of lemon zest

- ½ teaspoon of orange zest

- 2 tablespoons of olive oil

- 1 tablespoon of finely chopped fresh oregano leaves

- Salt to taste

- Black pepper to taste

- 2–3 tablespoons of freshly julienned mint leaves

Salad:

- 1 freshly diced medium-sized cucumber
- 2 cups of cooked and rinsed chickpeas
- ½ cup of freshly diced red onion
- 2 freshly diced medium-sized tomatoes
- 1 freshly diced red bell pepper
- ¼ cup of green olives
- ½ cup of pomegranates

Directions:

1. In a large salad bowl, add the juice and zest of both the lemon and the orange and oregano and olive oil. Whisk together so that they are mixed well. Season the vinaigrette with salt and pepper to taste.
2. After draining the chickpeas, add them to the dressing. Then add the onions. Give them a thorough mix, so that the onion and chickpeas absorb the flavors.
3. Now, chop the rest of the veggies and start adding them to the salad bowl. Give them a good toss.
4. Lastly, add the olives and fresh mint. Adjust the salt and pepper as required.

5. Serve this Mediterranean delight chilled—a cool summer salad that is good for the tummy and the soul.

Nutrition:

- **Calories: 286**
- **Carbohydrates: 29g**
- **Protein: 1g**
- **Fat: 11g**

26.   Tomato Gazpacho

Preparation time: 30 minutes.

Cooking time: 55 minutes.

Servings: 6

Ingredients:

- 2 tablespoons + 1 teaspoon red wine vinegar, divided

- ½ teaspoon pepper

- 1 teaspoon sea salt

- 1 avocado,

- ¼ cup basil, fresh & chopped

- 3 tablespoons + 2 teaspoons olive oil, divided

- 1 garlic clove, crushed

- 1 red bell pepper, sliced & seeded

- 1 cucumber, chunked

- 2(½) pounds large tomatoes, cored & chopped

Directions:

1. Place half of the cucumber, bell pepper, and ¼ cup of each tomato in a bowl, covering. Set it in the fried.
2. Puree your remaining tomatoes, cucumber, and bell pepper with garlic, 3 tablespoons of oil, 2 tablespoons of vinegar, sea salt, and black pepper into a blender, blending until smooth. Transfer it to a bowl and chill for 2 hours.
3. Chop the avocado, adding it to your chopped vegetables, adding the remaining oil, vinegar, salt, pepper, and basil.
4. Ladle the tomato puree mixture into bowls and serve with chopped vegetables as a salad.

Interesting facts: Avocados themselves are ranked within the top five of the healthiest foods on the planet, so you know that the oil produced from them is too. It is loaded with healthy fats and essential fatty acids. Like race bran oil, it is perfect to cook with as well! Bonus: Helps in the prevention of diabetes and lowers cholesterol levels.

Nutrition:

- **Calories: 201**
- **Protein: 23g**
- **Fat:4g**
- **Carbs: 2g**

27.   Vegetable Broth Sans Sodium

Preparation time: 5 minutes.

Cooking time: 60 minutes.

Servings: 1 cup.

Ingredients:

- 5 sprigs of dill
- 2 freshly sliced yellow onions
- 4 chives
- 6 freshly peeled and sliced carrots
- 10 cups of water
- 4 freshly sliced celery stalks
- 3 cloves of freshly minced garlic
- 4 sprigs of parsley

Directions:

1. Put a large pot on medium heat and stir the onions. Fry the onions for 1 minute until they become fragrant. Add the garlic, celery, carrots, and dill along with the chives and parsley, and cook everything. You will know that the mix is ready when it becomes fragrant.
2. Add the water and allow the mixture to a boil. Reduce the heat and allow everything to cook for 45 minutes.
3. Turn off the heat. The broth will cool in about 15 minutes.
4. Strain the broth with the help of a sieve so that you have a clear vegetable broth.
5. If you are not using the broth right away, store it as ice cubes. You can store the ice cubes for a week.

Nutrition:

- **Calories: 362**

- **Carbohydrates: 21g**

- **Protein: 12g**

- **Fat: 21g**

28.   African Pineapple Peanut Stew

Preparation time: 10 minutes.

Cooking time: 20 minutes.

Servings: 4

Ingredients:
- 4 cups sliced kale
- 1 cup chopped onion
- 1/2 cup peanut butter
- 1 tablespoon hot pepper sauce or 1 tablespoon Tabasco sauce
- 2 minced garlic cloves
- 1/2 cup chopped cilantro
- 2 cups pineapple, undrained, canned & crushed
- 1 tablespoon vegetable oil

Directions:

1. In a saucepan (preferably covered), sauté the garlic and onions in the oil until the onions are lightly browned, approximately 10 minutes, stirring often.
2. Wash the kale, till the time the onions are sautéed.
3. Get rid of the stems. Mound the leaves on a cutting surface & slice crosswise into slices (preferably 1" thick).
4. Now put the pineapple and juice to the onions & bring to a simmer. Stir the kale in, cover, and simmer until just tender, stirring frequently for approximately 5 minutes.
5. Mix in the hot pepper sauce, peanut butter & simmer for more than 5 minutes.
6. Add salt according to your taste.

Nutrition:

- **Calories: 402**

- **Carbohydrates: 7g**

- **Protein: 21g**

- **Fat: 34g**

29. Sweet Potato, Corn, and Jalapeno Bisque

Preparation time: 10 minutes.

Cooking time: 15 minutes.

Servings: 4

Ingredients:

- 4 ears corn
- 1 seeded and chopped jalapeno
- 4 cups vegetable broth
- 1 tablespoon olive oil
- 3 peeled and cubed sweet potatoes
- 1 chopped onion
- ½ tablespoon salt
- ¼ teaspoon black pepper
- 1 minced garlic clove

Directions:

1. In a pan, heat the oil over medium flame and sauté onion and garlic in it and cook for around 3 minutes. Put broth and sweet potatoes in it and bring it to a boil. Reduce the flame and cook it for an additional 10 minutes.

2. Remove it from the stove and blend it with a blender. Again, put it on the stove and add corn, jalapeno, salt, and black pepper and serve it.

Nutrition:

- **Carbohydrates 31g**

- **Protein 6g**

- **Fats 4g**

- **Sugar 11gg**

30.   Creamy Pea Soup with Olive Pesto

Preparation time: 20 minutes.

Cooking time: 20 minutes.

Servings: 4

Ingredients:

- 1 grated carrot
- 1 rinsed chopped leek
- 1 minced garlic clove
- 2 tablespoons olive oil
- 1 stem fresh thyme leaves
- 15 ounces rinsed and drained peas
- ½ tablespoon salt
- ¼ teaspoon ground black pepper
- 2(½) cups vegetable broth
- ¼ cup parsley leaves
- 1(¼) cup pitted green olives
- 1 teaspoon drained capers
- 1 garlic clove

Directions:

1. Take a pan with oil and put it over medium flame and whisk garlic, leek, thyme, and carrot in it. Cook it for around 4 minutes.
2. Add broth, peas, salt, and pepper, and increase the heat. When it starts boiling, lower down the heat and cook it with a lid on for around 15 minutes and remove from the heat and blend it.
3. For making pesto whisk parsley, olives, capers, and garlic and blend it in a way that it has little chunks. Top the soup with a scoop of olive pesto.

Nutrition:

- **Carbohydrates: 23g**
- **Protein: 6g**
- **Fats: 15g**
- **Sugar: 4g**
- **Calories: 230**

31.Cucumber Dill Gazpacho

Preparation time: 10 minutes

Cooking time: 2 hours

Servings: 4

Ingredients:

- 4 large cucumbers, peeled, deseeded, and chopped
- 1/8 teaspoon salt
- 1 teaspoon chopped fresh dill + more for garnishing
- 2 tablespoons freshly squeezed lemon juice
- 1(½) cups green grape, seeds removed
- 3 tablespoons extra-virgin olive oil
- 1 garlic clove, minced

Directions:

1. Add all the ingredients to a food processor and blend until smooth.
2. Pour the soup into serving bowls and chill for 1 to 2 hours.
3. Garnish with dill and serve chilled.

Nutrition:

- **Calories: 236**

- **Fat: 1.8g**

- **Carbs: 48.3g**

- **Protein: 7g**

32.   Moroccan Vegetable Stew

Preparation time: 5 minutes.

Cooking time: 35 minutes.

Servings: 4

Ingredients:

- 1 tablespoon olive oil

- 2 medium yellow onions, chopped

- 2 medium carrots, cut into 1/2-inch dice

- 1/2 teaspoon ground cumin

- 1/2 teaspoon ground cinnamon or allspice

- 1/2 teaspoon ground ginger

- 1/2 teaspoon sweet or smoked paprika

- 1/2 teaspoon saffron or turmeric

- 1(14.5-ounce) can diced tomatoes, undrained

- 8 ounces green beans, trimmed and cut into 1-inch pieces

- 2 cups peeled, seeded, and diced winter squash

- 1 large russet or another baking potato, peeled and cut into 1/2-inch dice

- 1(1/2) cups vegetable broth

- 11/2 cups cooked or 1(15.5-ounce) can chickpeas, drained and rinsed

- ¾ cup frozen peas

- 1/2 cup pitted dried plums (prunes)

- 1 teaspoon lemon zest

- Salt and freshly ground black pepper

- 1/2 cup pitted green olives

- 1 tablespoon minced fresh cilantro or parsley, for garnish

- 1/2 cup toasted slivered almonds, for garnish

Directions:
1. In a large saucepan, heat the oil over medium heat. Add the onions and carrots, cover, and cook for 5 minutes. Stir in cumin, cinnamon, ginger, paprika, and saffron. Cook, uncovered, stirring, for 30 seconds.
2. Add the tomatoes, green beans, squash, potato, and broth, and bring to a boil. Reduce heat to low, cover, and simmer until the vegetables are tender about 20 minutes.

3. Add the chickpeas, peas, dried plums, and lemon zest. Season with salt and pepper to taste. Stir in the olives and simmer, uncovered, until the flavors are blended for about 10 minutes. Sprinkle with cilantro and almonds and serve immediately.

Nutrition:

- **Calories: 71**
- **Fat: 2.8g**
- **Carbs: 9.8g**
- **Protein: 3.7g**

33. Basic Recipe for Vegetable Broth

Preparation time: 10 minutes.

Cooking time: 60 minutes.

Servings: Makes 2 quarts.

Ingredients:

- 8 cups water
- 1 onion, chopped
- 4 garlic cloves, crushed
- 2 celery stalks, chopped
- Pinch of salt
- 1 carrot, chopped
- Dash of pepper
- 1 potato, medium & chopped
- 1 tablespoon soy sauce
- 3 bay leaves

Directions:

1. To make the vegetable broth, you need to place all the ingredients in a deep saucepan.
2. Heat the pan over medium-high heat. Bring the vegetable mixture to a boil.
3. Once it starts boiling, lower the heat to medium-low and allow it to simmer for at least an hour or so. Cover it with a lid.
4. When the time is up, pass it through a filter and strain the vegetables, garlic, and bay leaves.
5. Allow the stock to cool completely and store in an air-tight container.

Nutrition:

- **Calories: 44**
- **Fat: 0.6g**
- **Carbs: 9.7g**
- **Protein: 0.9g**

34.   Garden Vegetable Stew

Preparation time: 5 minutes.

Cooking time: 60 minutes.

Servings: 4

Ingredients:

- 2 tablespoons olive oil
- 1 medium red onion, chopped
- 1 medium carrot, cut into 1/4-inch slices
- 1/2 cup dry white wine
- 3 medium new potatoes, unpeeled and cut into 1-inch pieces
- 1 medium red bell pepper, cut into 1/2-inch dice
- 1(1/2) cups vegetable broth
- 1 tablespoon minced fresh savory or 1 teaspoon dried

Directions:

1. In a large saucepan, heat the oil over medium heat. Add the onion and carrot, cover, and cook until softened, 7 minutes. Add the wine and cook, uncovered, for 5 minutes. Stir in the potatoes, bell pepper, and broth and bring to a boil. Reduce the heat to medium and simmer for 15 minutes.

2. Add the zucchini, yellow squash, and tomatoes. Season with salt and black pepper to taste, cover, and simmer until the vegetables are tender, 20 to 30 minutes. Stir in the corn, peas, basil, parsley, and savory. Taste, adjusting seasonings if necessary. Simmer to blend flavors about 10 minutes more. Serve immediately.

Nutrition:

- **Calories: 219**
- **Fat: 4.5g**
- **Carbs: 38.2g**
- **Protein: 6.4g**

35.   Spinach Soup with Dill and Basil

Preparation time: 10 minutes.

Cooking time: 25 minutes.

Servings: 8

Ingredients:

- 1-pound peeled and diced potatoes
- 1 tablespoon minced garlic
- 1 teaspoon dry mustard
- 6 cups vegetable broth
- 20 ounces chopped frozen spinach
- 2 cups chopped onion
- 1(½) tablespoon salt
- ½ cup minced dill
- 1 cup basil
- ½ teaspoon ground black pepper

Directions:

1. Whisk onion, garlic, potatoes, broth, mustard, and salt in a pan and cook it over medium flame. When it starts boiling, low down the heat and cover it with the lid and cook for 20 minutes.
2. Add the remaining ingredients in it and blend it; and cook it for few more minutes and serve it.

Nutrition:

- **Carbohydrates:12g**
- **Protein:13g**
- **Fats: 1g**
- **Calories: 165**

SOUP RECIPES

Soups

36.   Basil Tomato Soup

Preparation time: 10 minutes.

Cooking time: 10 minutes.

Servings: 6

Ingredients:

- 28 ounces can tomato
- ¼ cup basil pesto
- ¼ teaspoon dried basil leaves
- 1 teaspoon apple cider vinegar
- 2 tablespoons erythritol
- ¼ teaspoon garlic powder
- ½ teaspoon onion powder
- 2 cups water
- 1(½)teaspoon kosher salt

Directions:
1. Add tomatoes, garlic powder, onion powder, water, and salt to a saucepan.
2. Bring to a boil over medium heat. Reduce heat and simmer for 2 minutes.
3. Remove saucepan from heat and puree the soup using a blender until smooth.
4. Stir in pesto, dried basil, vinegar, and erythritol.
5. Stir well and serve warm.

Nutrition:

- **Calories: 662**

- **Carbohydrates: 18g**

- **Protein: 8g**

- **Fat: 55g**

37.   Cauliflower Asparagus Soup

Preparation time: 10 minutes.

Cooking time: 30 minutes.

Servings: 4

Ingredients:

- 20 asparagus spears, chopped
- 4 cups vegetable stock
- ½ cauliflower head, chopped
- 2 garlic cloves, chopped
- 1 tablespoon coconut oil
- Pepper to taste
- Salt to taste

Directions:

1. Heat coconut oil in a large saucepan over medium heat.
2. Add garlic and sauté until softened.
3. Add cauliflower, vegetable stock, pepper, and salt. Stir well and bring to a boil.
4. Reduce heat to low and simmer for 20 minutes.
5. Add chopped asparagus and cook until softened.
6. Puree the soup using an immersion blender until smooth and creamy.
7. Stir well and serve warm.

Nutrition:

- **Calories: 298**
- **Carbohydrates: 26g**
- **Protein: 21g**
- **Fat: 9g**

38.   Mushroom & Broccoli Soup

Preparation time: 20 minutes.

Cooking time: 45 minutes.

Servings: 8

Ingredients:

- 1 bundle broccoli (around 1–1/2 pounds)
- 1 tablespoon canola oil
- 1/2 pound cut crisp mushrooms
- 1 tablespoon diminished sodium soy sauce
- 2 medium carrots, finely slashed
- 2 celery ribs, finely slashed
- 1/4 cup finely slashed onion
- 1 garlic clove, minced
- 1 container (32 ounces) vegetable juices
- 2 cups of water
- 2 tablespoons lemon juice

Directions:

1. Cut broccoli florets into reduced-down pieces. Strip and hack stalks.
2. In an enormous pot, heat oil over medium-high warmth; sauté mushrooms until delicate, 4–6 minutes. Mix in soy sauce; expel from skillet.
3. In the same container, join broccoli stalks, carrots, celery, onion, garlic, soup, and water; heat to the point of boiling. Diminish heat; stew, revealed, until vegetables are relaxed, 25–30 minutes.
4. Puree soup utilizing a drenching blender. Or then again, cool marginally, puree the soup in a blender; come back to the dish.
5. Mix in florets and mushrooms; heat to the point of boiling. Lessen warmth to medium; cook until broccoli is delicate, 8–10 minutes, blending infrequently. Mix in lemon juice.

Nutrition:

- **Calories: 830**

- **Carbohydrates: 8g**

- **Protein: 45g**

- **Fat: 64g**

39. Garden Vegetable and Herb Soup

Preparation time: 20 minutes.

Cooking time: 30 minutes.

Servings: 8

Ingredients:

- 2 tablespoons olive oil
- 2 medium onions, hacked
- 2 huge carrots, cut
- 1-pound red potatoes (around 3 medium), cubed
- 2 cups of water
- 1 can (14–1/2 ounces) diced tomatoes in sauce
- 1–1/2 cups vegetable soup
- 1–1/2 teaspoons garlic powder
- 1 teaspoon dried basil
- 1/2 teaspoon salt
- 1/2 teaspoon paprika
- 1/4 teaspoon dill weed
- 1/4 teaspoon pepper
- 1 medium yellow summer squash, split and cut
- 1 medium zucchini, split and cut

Directions:

1. In a huge pan, heat oil over medium warmth. Include onions and carrots; cook and mix until onions are delicate, 4–6 minutes. Include potatoes and cook for 2 minutes. Mix in water, tomatoes, juices, and seasonings.
2. Heat to the point of boiling. Diminish heat; stew, revealed, until potatoes and carrots are tender, 9 minutes.
3. Add yellow squash and zucchini; cook until vegetables are tender, 9 minutes longer. Serve or, whenever wanted, puree blend in clusters, including extra stock until desired consistency is accomplished.

Nutrition:

- **Calories: 252**
- **Carbohydrates: 12g**
- **Protein: 1g**
- **Fat: 11g**

40.   Tomato Pumpkin Soup

Preparation time: 25 minutes.

Cooking time: 25 minutes.

Servings: 4

Ingredients:

- 2 cups pumpkin, diced
- 1/2 cup tomato, chopped
- 1/2 cup onion, chopped
- 1(1/2) teaspoon curry powder
- 1/2 teaspoon paprika
- 2 cups vegetable stock
- 1 teaspoon olive oil
- 1/2 teaspoon garlic, minced

Directions:

1. In a saucepan, add oil, garlic, and onion and sauté for 3 minutes over medium heat.
2. Add the remaining ingredients into the saucepan and bring to a boil.
3. Reduce heat and cover and simmer for 10 minutes.
4. Puree the soup using a blender until smooth.
5. Stir well and serve warm.

Nutrition:

- **Calories: 340**
- **Protein: 50g**
- **Carbohydrate: 14g**
- **Fat: 10g**

41.Creamy Cauliflower Pakora Soup

Preparation time: 20 minutes.

Cooking time: 20 minutes.

Servings: 8

Ingredients:

- 1 huge head cauliflower, cut into little florets
- 5 medium potatoes, stripped and diced
- 1 huge onion, diced
- 4 medium carrots, stripped and diced
- 2 celery ribs, diced
- 1 container (32 ounces) vegetable stock
- 1 teaspoon garam masala
- 1 teaspoon garlic powder
- 1 teaspoon ground coriander
- 1 teaspoon ground turmeric
- 1 teaspoon ground cumin
- 1 teaspoon pepper
- 1 teaspoon salt
- 1/2 teaspoon squashed red pepper chips
- Water or extra vegetable stock
- New cilantro leaves for serving
- Lime wedges, discretionary

Directions:

1. In a Dutch stove over medium-high warmth, heat the initial 14 ingredients to the point of boiling. Cook and mix until vegetables are delicate, around 20 minutes. Expel from heat; cool marginally. Process in groups in a blender or nourishment processor until smooth. Modify consistency as wanted with water (or extra stock). Sprinkle with new cilantro. Serve hot with lime wedges whenever wanted.

2. Stop alternative: Before including cilantro, solidify cooled soup in cooler compartments. To utilize, in part defrost in cooler medium-term.

3. Warmth through in a pan, blending every so often and adding a little water if fundamental. Sprinkle with cilantro. Whenever wanted, present with lime wedges.

Nutrition:
- **Calories: 248**
- **Carbohydrates: 7g**
- **Protein: 1g**
- **Fat: 19g**

42.   Green Spinach Kale Soup

Preparation time: 10 minutes.

Cooking time: 5 minutes.

Servings: 6

Ingredients:

- 2 avocados
- 8 ounces spinach
- 8 ounces kale
- 1 fresh lime juice
- 1 cup water
- 3(1/3) cup coconut milk
- 3 ounces olive oil
- 1/4 teaspoon pepper
- 1 teaspoon salt

Directions:
1. Heat olive oil in a saucepan over medium heat.
2. Add kale and spinach to the saucepan and sauté for 2–3 minutes. Remove saucepan from heat. Add coconut milk, spices, avocado, and water. Stir well.
3. Puree the soup using an immersion blender until smooth and creamy. Add fresh lime juice and stir well.
4. Serve and enjoy!

Nutrition:

- **Calories: 312**
- **Protein: 9g**
- **Fat: 10g**
- **Carbs: 22g**

43.   Amazing Chickpea and Noodle Soup

Preparation time: 10 minutes.
Cooking time: 20 minutes.
Servings: 1 cup.

Ingredients:
- 1 freshly diced celery stalk
- ¼ cup of 'chicken' seasoning
- 1 cup of freshly diced onion
- 3 cloves of freshly crushed garlic
- 2 cups of cooked chickpeas
- 4 cups of vegetable broth
- Freshly chopped cilantro for serving
- 2 freshly cubed medium-size potatoes
- Salt to taste
- 2 freshly sliced carrots
- ½ teaspoon of dried thyme
- Pepper to taste
- 2 cups of water
- 6 ounces of gluten-free spaghetti

'Chicken' seasoning:
- 1 tablespoon of garlic powder
- 2 teaspoons of sea salt

- 1(1/3) cup of nutritional yeast
- 3 tablespoons of onion powder
- 1 teaspoon of oregano
- ½ teaspoon of turmeric
- 1(½) tablespoon of dried basil

Directions:
1. Put a pot on medium heat and sauté the onion. It will soften within 3 minutes.
2. Add celery, potato, and carrots and sauté for another 3 minutes.
3. Add the 'chicken' seasoning to the garlic, thyme, water, and vegetable broth.
4. Simmer the mix on medium-high heat. Cook the veggies for about 20 minutes until they soften.
5. Add the cooked pasta and chickpeas.
6. Add salt and pepper to taste.
7. Put the fresh cilantro on top and enjoy the fresh soup!

Nutrition:
- **Calories: 405**
- **Carbohydrates: 1g**
- **Protein: 19g**
- **Fat: 38g**

44.   Vegan Way Lentil Soup

Preparation time: 5 minutes.

Cooking time: 20 minutes.

Servings: 1 cup.

Ingredients:

- 2 tablespoons of water
- 4 stalks of thinly sliced celery
- 2 cloves of freshly minced garlic
- 4 thinly sliced large carrots
- Sea salt to taste
- 2 freshly diced small shallots
- Pepper to taste
- 3 cups of red/yellow baby potatoes
- 2 cups of chopped sturdy greens
- 4 cups of vegetable broth
- 1 cup of uncooked brown or green lentils
- ½ teaspoon Fresh rosemary/thyme

Directions:

1. Put a large pot over medium heat. Once the pot is hot enough, add the shallots, garlic, celery, and carrots to water. Season the veggies with a little bit of pepper and salt.

2. Sauté the veggies for 5 minutes until they are tender. You will know that the veggies are ready when they have turned golden brown. Be careful with the garlic, because it can easily burn.

3. Add the potatoes and some more seasoning. Cook for 2 minutes.

4. Mix the vegetable broth with the rosemary. Now Increase the heat to medium-high. Allow the veggies to be on a rolling simmer. Add the lentils and give everything a thorough stir.

5. Once it starts to simmer again, decrease the heat and simmer for about 20 minutes without a cover. You will know that the veggies are ready when both the lentils and potatoes are soft

6. Add the greens. Cook for 4 minutes until they wilt. You can adjust the flavor with seasonings.

7. Enjoy this with rice or flatbread. The leftovers are equally tasty, so store them well to enjoy on a day when you are not in the mood to cook.

Nutrition:

- Calories: 284
- Carbohydrates: 21g
- Protein: 11g
- Fat: 19g

45.   Roasted Red Pepper and Butternut Squash Soup

Preparation time: 10 minutes.

Cooking time: 45 minutes.

Servings: 6

Ingredients:

- 1 small butternut squash
- 1 tablespoon olive oil
- 1 teaspoon sea salt
- 2 red bell peppers
- 1 yellow onion
- 1 head garlic
- 2 cups water, or vegetable broth
- Zest and juice of 1 lime
- 1 to 2 tablespoons tahini
- Pinch cayenne pepper
- ½ teaspoon ground coriander
- ½ teaspoon ground cumin
- Toasted squash seeds (optional)

Directions:

1. Preheat the oven to 350°F.

2. Prepare the squash for roasting by cutting it in half lengthwise, scooping out the seeds, and poking holes in the flesh with a fork. Reserve the seeds if desired.

3. Rub a small amount of oil over the flesh and skin, rub with a bit of sea salt, and put the halves skin-side down in a large baking dish. Put it in the oven while you prepare the rest of the vegetables.

4. Prepare the peppers the same way, except they do not need to be poked.

5. Slice the onion in half and rub oil on the exposed faces. Slice the top off the head of garlic and rub oil on the exposed flesh.

6. After the squash has cooked for 20 minutes, add the peppers, onion, and garlic, and roast for another 20 minutes. Optionally, you can toast the squash seeds by putting them in the oven in a separate baking dish 10 to 15 minutes before the vegetables are finished.

7. Keep a close eye on them. When the vegetables are cooked, take them out and let them cool before handling them. The squash will be very soft when poked with a fork.

8. Scoop the flesh out of the squash skin into a large pot (if you have an immersion blender) or into a blender.

9. Chop the pepper roughly, remove the onion skin and chop the onion roughly, and squeeze the garlic

cloves out of the head, all into the pot or blender. Add the water, the lime zest and juice, and the tahini. Purée the soup, adding more water if you like, to your desired consistency. Season with salt, cayenne, coriander, and cumin. Serve garnished with toasted squash seeds (if using).

Nutrition:

- **Calories: 156**
- **Protein: 4g**
- **Total fat: 7g**
- **Saturated fat: 11g**
- **Carbohydrates: 22g**
- **Fiber: 5g**

46.   Coconut Watercress Soup

Preparation time: 10 minutes.

Cooking time: 20 minutes.

Servings: 4

Ingredients:

- 1 teaspoon coconut oil
- 1 onion, diced
- ¾ cup coconut milk
- 2 ounce Peas
- 1 cup Water
- 1 cup Watercress
- 1 ounce Mint
- Salt and pepper to taste

Directions:

1. Melt the coconut oil in a large pot over medium-high heat. Add the onion and cook until soft about 5 minutes, then add the peas and the water. Bring to a boil, lower the heat and add the watercress, mint, salt, and pepper.
2. Cover and simmer for 5 minutes. Stir in the coconut milk, and purée the soup until smooth in a blender or with an immersion blender.
3. Try this soup with any other fresh, leafy green— anything from spinach to collard greens to arugula to Swiss chard.

Nutrition:

- **Calories: 160**
- **Fat: 5g**
- **Carbs: 25g**
- **Proteins: 2g**

47. Avocado Mint Soup

Preparation time: 10 minutes.

Cooking time: 10 minutes.

Servings: 2

Ingredients:

- 1 medium avocado, peeled, pitted, and cut into pieces
- 1 cup coconut milk
- 2 romaine lettuce leaves
- 20 fresh mint leaves
- 1 tablespoon fresh lime juice
- 1/8 teaspoon salt

Directions:

1. Add all the ingredients into the blender and blend until smooth. The soup should be thick not as a puree.
2. Pour into the serving bowls and place them in the refrigerator for 10 minutes.
3. Stir well and serve chilled.

Nutrition:

- **Calories: 377**
- **Fat: 14.9g**
- **Carbs: 60.7g**
- **Protein: 6.4g**

48.   Cauliflower Spinach Soup

Preparation time: 30 minutes.

Cooking time: 25 minutes.

Servings: 5

Ingredients:

- 1/2 cup unsweetened coconut milk
- 5 ounces fresh spinach, chopped
- 5 watercress, chopped
- 8 cups vegetable stock
- 1-pound cauliflower, chopped
- Salt to taste

Directions:

1. Add stock and cauliflower in a large saucepan and bring to a boil over medium heat for 15 minutes.
2. Add spinach and watercress and cook for another 10 minutes.
3. Remove from the heat and puree the soup using a blender until smooth.
4. Add coconut milk and stir well. Season with salt.
5. Stir well and serve hot.

Nutrition:

- **Calories: 271**

- **Fat: 3.7g**

- **Carbs: 54g**

- **Proteins: 6.5g**

49.   Creamy Squash Soup

Preparation time: 10 minutes.

Cooking time: 25 minutes.

Servings: 8

Ingredients:

- 3 cups butternut squash, chopped
- 1(½) cups unsweetened coconut milk
- 1 tablespoon coconut oil
- 1 teaspoon dried onion flakes
- 1 tablespoon curry powder
- 4 cups water
- 1 garlic clove
- 1 teaspoon kosher salt

Directions:

1. Add squash, coconut oil, onion flakes, curry powder, water, garlic, and salt into a large saucepan. Bring to a boil over high heat.
2. Turn heat to medium and simmer for 20 minutes.
3. Puree the soup using a blender until smooth. Return soup to the saucepan and stir in coconut milk and cook for 2 minutes.
4. Stir well and serve hot.

Nutrition:

- **Calories: 271**
- **Fat: 3.7g**
- **Carbs: 54g**
- **Protein:6.5g**

50.   Zucchini Soup

Preparation time: 10 minutes.

Cooking time: 15 minutes.

Servings: 8

Ingredients:

- 2(½)pounds zucchini, peeled and sliced
- 1/3 cup basil leaves
- 4 cups vegetable stock
- 4 garlic cloves, chopped
- 2 tablespoons olive oil
- 1 medium onion, diced
- Pepper to taste
- Salt to taste

Directions:

1. Heat olive oil in a pan over medium-low heat.
2. Add zucchini and onion and sauté until softened. Add garlic and sauté for a minute.
3. Add vegetable stock and simmer for 15 minutes.
4. Remove from the heat. Stir in basil and puree the soup using a blender until smooth and creamy. Season with pepper and salt.
5. Stir well and serve.

Nutrition:

- **Calories: 434**

- **Fat: 35g**

- **Carbs: 27g**

- **Protein: 6.7g**

51.Avocado Cucumber Soup

Preparation time: 20 minutes.

Cooking time: 0 minutes.

Servings: 3

Ingredients:

- 1 large cucumber, peeled and sliced
- ¾ cup water
- ¼ cup lemon juice
- 2 garlic cloves
- 6 green onion
- 2 avocados, pitted
- ½ teaspoon black pepper
- ½ teaspoon pink salt

Directions:

1. Add all the ingredients into the blender and blend until smooth and creamy.
2. Place in the refrigerator for 30 minutes.
3. Stir well and serve chilled.

Nutrition:

- **Calories: 127**
- **Fat: 6.6g**
- **Carbs: 13g**
- **Protein: 0.7g**

52. Creamy Celery Soup

Preparation time: 20 minutes.

Cooking time: 20 minutes.

Servings: 4

Ingredients:

- 6 cups celery
- ½ teaspoon dill
- 2 cups water
- 1 cup coconut milk
- 1 onion, chopped
- Pinch of salt

Directions:

1. Add all the ingredients into the electric pot and stir well.
2. Cover electric pot with the lid and select soup setting.
3. Release pressure using a quick-release method, then open the lid.
4. Puree the soup using an immersion blender until smooth and creamy.
5. Stir well and serve warm.

Nutrition:

- **Calories: 159**
- **Fat: 8.4g**
- **Carbs: 19.8g**
- **Proteins: 4.6g**

53.   Moroccan Vermicelli Vegetable Soup

Preparation time: 5 minutes.

Cooking time: 35 minutes.

Servings: 4 to 6

Ingredients:

- 1 tablespoon olive oil
- 1 small onion, chopped
- 1 large carrot, chopped
- 1 celery rib, chopped
- 3 small zucchinis, cut into 1/4-inch dice
- 1 (28-ounce) can diced tomatoes, drained
- 2 tablespoons tomato paste
- 1(1/2) cups cooked or 1 (15.5-ounce) can chickpeas, drained and rinsed
- 2 teaspoons smoked paprika
- 1 teaspoon ground cumin
- 1 teaspoon za'atar spice (optional)
- 1/4 teaspoon ground cayenne

- 6 cups vegetable broth, homemade (see light vegetable broth) or store-bought, or water

- Salt to taste

- 4 ounces vermicelli

- 2 tablespoons minced fresh cilantro, for garnish

Directions:

1. In a large soup pot, heat the oil over medium heat. Add the onion, carrot, and celery. Cover and cook until softened, about 5 minutes. Stir in the zucchini, tomatoes, tomato paste, chickpeas, paprika, cumin, za'atar, and cayenne.
2. Add the broth and salt to taste. Bring to a boil, then reduce heat to low and simmer, uncovered, until the vegetables are tender about 30 minutes.
3. Shortly before serving, stir in the vermicelli and cook until the noodles are tender about 5 minutes. Ladle the soup into bowls, garnish with cilantro, and serve.

Nutrition:

- **Calories: 236**

- **Fat: 1.8g**

- **Carbs: 48.3g**

- **Protein: 7g**

54.   Red Lentil Soup

Preparation time: 5 minutes.

Cooking time: 25 minutes.

Servings: Makes 6 cups.

Ingredients:

- 2 tablespoons nutritional yeast
- 1 cup red lentil, washed
- ½ tablespoon garlic, minced
- 4 cups vegetable stock
- 1 teaspoon salt
- 2 cups kale, shredded
- 3 cups mixed vegetables

Directions:

1. To start with, place all the ingredients needed to make the soup in a large pot.
2. Heat the pot over medium-high heat and bring the mixture to a boil.
3. Once it starts boiling, lower the heat to low. Allow the soup to simmer.
4. Simmer it for 1o to 15 minutes or until cooked.
5. Serve and enjoy!

Nutrition:

- **Calories: 212**

- **Fat: 11.9g**

- **Carbs: 31.7g**

- **Protein: 7.3g**

55.   Coconut and Grilled Vegetable Soup

Preparation time: 10 minutes.

Cooking time: 45 minutes.

Servings: 4

Ingredients:

- 2 small red onions cut into wedges
- 2 garlic cloves
- 10 ounces butternut squash, peeled and chopped
- 10 ounces pumpkins, peeled and chopped
- 4 tablespoon melted vegan butter
- Salt and black pepper to taste
- 1 cup of water
- 1 cup unsweetened coconut milk
- 1 lime juiced
- ¾ cup vegan mayonnaise
- Toasted pumpkin seeds for garnishing

Directions:

1. Preheat the oven to 400°F.
2. On a baking sheet, spread the onions, garlic, butternut squash, and pumpkins and drizzle half of the butter on top. Season with salt, black pepper, and rub the seasoning well into the vegetables. Roast in the oven for 45 minutes or until the vegetables are golden brown and softened.
3. Transfer the vegetables to a pot; add the remaining ingredients except for the pumpkin seeds and using an immersion blender, puree the ingredients until smooth.
4. Dish the soup, garnish with the pumpkin seeds and serve warm.

Nutrition:

- **Calories: 290**
- **Fat:10g**
- **Protein:30g**
- **Carbohydrates: 0g**

56.   Celery Dill Soup

Preparation time: 5 minutes.

Cooking time: 25 minutes.

Servings: 4

Ingredients:

- 2 tablespoon coconut oil
- ½ pound celery root, trimmed
- 1 garlic clove
- 1 medium white onion
- ¼ cup fresh dill, roughly chopped
- 1 teaspoon cumin powder
- ¼ teaspoon nutmeg powder
- 1 small head cauliflower, cut into florets
- 3(½) cups seasoned vegetable stock
- 5 ounces vegan butter
- Juice from 1 lemon
- ¼ cup coconut cream
- Salt and black pepper to taste

Directions:

1. Melt the coconut oil in a large pot and sauté the celery root, garlic, and onion until softened and fragrant, 5 minutes.
2. Stir in the dill, cumin, and nutmeg, and stir-fry for 1 minute. Mix in the cauliflower and vegetable stock. Allow the soup to a boil for 15 minutes and turn the heat off.
3. Add the vegan butter and lemon juice, and puree the soup using an immersion blender.
4. Stir in the coconut cream, salt, black pepper, and dish the soup.
5. Serve warm.

Nutrition:

- **Calories: 320**
- **Fat:10g**
- **Protein:20g**
- **Carbohydrates: 30g**

57.   Broccoli Fennel Soup

Preparation time: 15 minutes.

Cooking time: 10 minutes.

Servings: 4

Ingredients:

- 1 fennel bulb, white and green parts coarsely chopped
- 10 ounces broccoli, cut into florets
- 3 cups vegetable stock
- Salt and freshly ground black pepper
- 1 garlic clove
- 1 cup dairy-free cream cheese
- 3 ounces vegan butter
- ½ cup chopped fresh oregano

Directions:

1. In a medium pot, combine the fennel, broccoli, vegetable stock, salt, and black pepper. Bring to a boil until the vegetables soften, 10 to 15 minutes.
2. Stir in the remaining ingredients and simmer the soup for 3 to 5 minutes.
3. Adjust the taste with salt and black pepper, and dish the soup.
4. Serve warm.

Nutrition:

- **Calories:240**

- **Fat: 0g**

- **Protein:0g**

- **Carbohydrates:20g**

58. Spinach and Kale Soup

Preparation time: 5 minutes.

Cooking time: 5 minutes.

Servings: 2

Ingredients:

- 3 ounces vegan butter
- 1 cup fresh spinach, chopped coarsely
- 1 cup fresh kale, chopped coarsely
- 1 large avocado
- 3 tablespoons chopped fresh mint leaves
- 3(½) cups coconut cream
- 1 cup vegetable broth
- Salt and black pepper to taste
- 1 lime, juiced

Directions:

1. Melt the vegan butter in a medium pot over medium heat and sauté the kale and spinach until wilted, 3 minutes. Turn the heat off.
2. Stir in the remaining ingredients and using an immersion blender, puree the soup until smooth.
3. Dish the soup and serve warm.

Nutrition:

- **Calories: 380**

- **Fat: 10g**

- **Protein: 20g**

- **Carbohydrates: 30g**

59.   Tofu and Mushroom Soup

Preparation time: 15 minutes.

Cooking time: 10 minutes.

Servings: 4

Ingredients:

- 2 tablespoons olive oil
- 1 garlic clove, minced
- 1 large yellow onion, finely chopped
- 1 teaspoon freshly grated ginger
- 1 cup vegetable stock
- 2 small potatoes, peeled and chopped
- ¼ teaspoon salt
- ¼ teaspoon black pepper
- 2(14-ounces) silken tofu, drained and rinsed
- 2/3 cup baby Bella mushrooms, sliced
- 1 tablespoon chopped fresh oregano
- 2 tablespoons chopped fresh parsley to garnish

Directions:

1. Heat the olive oil in a medium pot over medium heat and sauté the garlic, onion, and ginger until soft and fragrant.

2. Pour in the vegetable stock, potatoes, salt, and black pepper. Cook until the potatoes soften, 12 minutes.

3. Stir in the tofu and using an immersion blender, puree the ingredients until smooth.

4. Mix in the mushrooms and simmer with the pot covered until the mushrooms warm up while occasionally stirring to ensure that the tofu doesn't curdle for 7 minutes.

5. Stir oregano and dish the soup.

6. Garnish with the parsley and serve warm.

Nutrition:

- **Calories:310**
- **Fat:10g**
- **Protein:40.0g**
- **Carbohydrates: 0g**

60.   Pesto Pea Soup

Preparation time: 10 minutes.
Cooking time: 20 minutes.
Servings: 4

Ingredients:

- 2 cups water
- 8 ounces tortellini
- ¼ cup pesto
- 1 onion, small & finely chopped
- 1-pound peas, frozen
- 1 carrot, medium & finely chopped
- 1(¾) cup vegetable broth, less sodium
- 1 celery rib, medium & finely chopped

Directions:

1. To start with, boil the water in a large pot over medium-high heat.
2. Next, stir in the tortellini to the pot and cook it following the packet's instructions.
3. In the meantime, cook the onion, celery, and carrot in a deep saucepan along with the water and broth.
4. Cook the celery and onion mixture for 6 minutes or until softened.

5. Now, spoon in the peas and allow them to simmer while keeping them uncovered.

6. Cook the peas for few minutes or until they are bright green and soft.

7. Then spoon in the pesto to the pea's mixture. Combine well.

8. Pour the mixture into a high-speed blender and blend for 2 to 3 minutes or until you get a rich, smooth soup.

9. Return the soup to the pan. Spoon in the cooked tortellini.

10. Finally, pour into a serving bowl and top with more cooked peas if desired.

11. **Tip:** If desired, you can season it with Maldon salt at the end.

Nutrition:
- **Calories:100**
- **Fat: 0g**
- **Protein: 0g**
- **Carbohydrates: 0g**

61.Tofu Goulash Soup

Preparation time: 35 minutes.

Cooking time: 20 minutes.

Servings: 4

Ingredients:

- 4(¼-ounces) vegan butter
- 1 white onion, chopped
- 2 garlic cloves, minced
- 1(½) cups butternut squash
- 1 red bell pepper, deseeded and chopped
- 1 tablespoon paprika powder
- ¼ teaspoon red chili flakes
- 1 tablespoon dried basil
- ½ tablespoon crushed cardamom seeds
- Salt and black pepper to taste
- 1(½) cups crushed tomatoes
- 3 cups vegetable broth
- 1(½)teaspoon red wine vinegar
- Chopped parsley to serve

Directions:

1. Place the tofu between 2 paper towels and allow the draining of water for 30 minutes. After, crumble the tofu and set it aside.
2. Melt the vegan butter in a large pot over medium heat and sauté the onion and garlic until the veggies are fragrant and soft, 3 minutes.
3. Stir in the tofu and cook until golden brown, 3 minutes.
4. Add the butternut squash, bell pepper, paprika, red chili flakes, basil, cardamom seeds, salt, and black pepper. Cook for 2 minutes to release some flavor and mix in the tomatoes and 2 cups of vegetable broth.
5. Close the lid, bring the soup to a boil, and then simmer for 10 minutes.
6. Stir in the remaining vegetable broth, the red wine vinegar, and adjust the taste with salt and black pepper.
7. Dish the soup, garnish with the parsley and serve warm.

Nutrition:

- **Calories:320**
- **Fat:10g**
- **Protein:10g**
- **Carbohydrates: 20g**

Conclusion

Regarding the alkaline diet there are conflicting opinions, as with all types of diets.

Most people confuse acidic and alkalizing foods with the concept of the pH of the food. So, according to this wrong view, lemon juice would be a particularly acid food, when in fact it is one of the most known alkalizing foods, so much that it is even recommended in therapy to alkalize urine and prevent the formation of kidney stones.

The alkalinity or acidity of a food is attributed not according to the pH of the food itself, but according to the pH of the solution in which its ashes are dispersed, therefore according to the pH of inorganic residues, not metabolized by the body. Thus, to resume the example of lemon, the organic acids which determine the acidity of this food are metabolized by the organism, whereas the basic inorganic residues are excreted unmodified with urine, basifying them.

Besides the many theories on which it has been built, the alkaline diet has the merit of promoting the consumption of fresh vegetables, often lacking in the western diet compared to what recommended by nutritionists, and of discouraging the consumption - often excessive - of meat, sausages, salami, simple sugars and alcohol.

Scrolling down the list of the most known alkalizing and alkaline foods, it can be understood how a similar food model can actually promote the health of the organism, with evident and immediate benefits in the passage from a typical western diet to the alkalizing one.

In conclusion, a Plant Based diet based on alkaline foods offers many benefits and, thanks to the recipes in this book, you'll get to experience it for yourself.

If you enjoyed the recipes included in this book and you want to try others, you can find them in the books of the same series. They are:

In the same series you can find:

PLANT BASED DIET: THE BENEFITS

PLANT BASED DIET COOKBOOK: RECIPES FOR YOUR BREAKFAST

PLANT BASED DIET COOKBOOK: RECIPES FOR YOUR LUNCH

PLANT BASED DIET COOKBOOK: RECIPES FOR YOUR DINNER

PLANT BASED DIET COOKBOOK: RECIPES FOR YOUR SALADS

PLANT BASED DIET COOKBOOK: RECIPES FOR YOUR DESSERTS

PLANT BASED DIET COOKBOOK: SUPERFOODS RECIPES

PLANT BASED DIET COOKBOOK: RECIPES FOR YOUR JUICES&SMOOTHIES

CPSIA information can be obtained
at www.ICGtesting.com
Printed in the USA
LVHW081931220821
695845LV00001B/70